"In *Profeta Without Refuge*, Leon writes: 'Life requires a haunting' and then proceeds to do exactly this by creating a world that acts like a veil to the one we reside in. She has forced a parallel seeing: Black bodies lying in the streets and the constant naming of such violence with the remembering of who we are as a people, our ancestral and godlike abilities, our world full of mysticism and energy. 'Black people have no futures / in sci-fi or horror,' she writes, and yet within the compounds of this text we know that this type of escapism might be the only place where we can safely create our (r)evolutions. This is an ambitious and profoundly beautiful work that will stay with me the rest of my days."

– Yesenia Montilla author of *The Pink Box* (2015),
longlisted for the Pen Open Book Award 2016

"Chilling, raw, honest, and brave enough to be felt under the skin, Leon's aesthetically well-crafted poems in *Profeta Without Refuge* filled my body with the breath it's been looking for since the deaths of Trayvon Martin, Eric Garner, and Sandra Bland.

These lyrical and experimental poems explore the belief that our bodies are containers of trauma. Whether passed on from one generation to the next or lived in the flesh, the fear, heartbreak, violence, suffering, and anxiety become a part of us and ultimately shape who and what we are and can become. With precise language, eloquent musicality, and harrowing mysticism and metaphor, Raina J. León is able to articulate both the historical and current suffering experienced by the Black community in America. These poems are inescapable, they hold us captive and demand our attention on the page. Whether we move our eyes from left to right, right to left, or up and down each line, or pick up our cell phones to interact with the text in poems like 'code,' she is reminding us that our skin, our body, our blood, and our bones hold and respond to physical and emotional trauma that cannot / should not be forgotten or erased."

– Jasminne Mendez, International Latino Book Award winner, *Island of Dreams* (2013)

10/29/18

Dear Ingrid,
Thank you so much
for honoring my work
and loved experiences –
your words such
significant & resonant
of my truths
& experiences.

Siempre p'alante
Raina

Profeta Without Refuge

Raina J. León

Nomadic Press
2016

This book was made possible by a loving community of family and friends, old and new.

Requests for permission to make copies of any part of the work should be sent to
info@nomadicpress.org.

For author questions or to book a reading at your school, bookstore, or alternative
establishment, please send an email to info@nomadicpress.org.

Published by Nomadic Press, 2926 Foothill Boulevard, Oakland, California, 94601
www.nomadicpress.org

First Edition
First Printing

Printed in the United States

Library of Congress Cataloging-in-Publication Data

León, Raina J. 1981 –
Profeta Without Refuge / written by Raina J. León; illustrated by Arthur Johnstone and
Livien Yin
p. cm.
Summary: *Profeta Without Refuge* engages in poetic experimentation through the writing
of an Afrocentric and womanist creation myth in resistance to state-sanctioned violence
against Black and brown peoples. The book includes poems in the voices of three
characters: the creator goddess of a Black immortal people; her human daughter who carries
the vivid memories of generational trauma and joy; and the poet who serves as witness to
reality and creator of the surreal as survival mechanism in our tumultuous times.
[1. POETRY / Subjects & Themes / Race. 2. POETRY / Subjects & Themes / Trauma. 3.
POETRY / American / Violence.] I. Title.

2016953749

ISBN: 978-0-9981348-0-2

The illustrations in this book were created using pen and marker on Canson paper.
The type was set in Garamond Premier Pro.
Printed and bound in the United States
Typesetting and book design by J. K. Fowler
Edited by Arisa White and J. K. Fowler

for the living and the dead

for the joyful and the mourning

for matteo, norma, eddie, maryann, pat, clifton, and all the family not listed and the friends who are family, all who see me when the threat of erasure is real

CONTENTS

THE POET ENTERS AND THEY LEAVE

picture

i release poems to breath

podium

theater burn-lights

see myself multiple
three shadows
& i know

not mine not mine not mine but
      slave elisha wanting former & latter dreaming
             his tongue on god's thumb   suck   long long live
        suffering in their twining   a hol(y) (k)new   (not)
persephone means destruction
destroy murder
the body
so many black & brown bodies
devil-delivered
and they say reasonable
tamir
spirit, name say his,
how do i stop shaking

i read their voices
      barriers to my shatter
conjure them awakening   & somewhere
myrrh

i remember my skin pebbled over

a door
closed & opened & closed

NOTES

There are 12 characters, only three of which appear here, identified by *italics*:

1. iset: *origin of the African immortals. She comes from a tribe of people devoted to the sanctity of death. They were the myrrh and frankincense gatherers. They performed rites that promised a peaceful communion with death. Their art was focused on the ushering of men with no people; women were healed, lived long, died surrounded by other women. In her matriarchal and matrilineal tribe, her mother was knowledge-carrier of all rites. The rape of iset and the killing of her people in a river leads to the creation of a reverse watershed. The spirits of the dead, those in the original tribe and all those who are ushered into death, persist within her and all those she creates. Water from the source river, tainted as it is with suspended blood ribbons, creates new immortals. It is guarded by hulda. Immortals do age, can have children, but they can only die and their spirits return to ether by burning at the source water. Otherwise, their spirits remain in this world even after the body dies. Source water can also slow aging. Though 5,000 years old, iset looks as if she is in middle age. Her poems often offer an official story and a subjective story. iset carries more spirits and shifts in personality because of her position as origin god.*

2. hulda: one of the sisters of iset, first in creation. She was given immortality as a child but looks as if she is in her 80s as she only rarely takes source water, which slows the aging process but does not stop it. She prefers to give her portion to another each year as a part of her commitment to healing. Immortals receive the vial of source water, deemed a sacred gift, once every hundred years. hulda uses her vial sparingly over that time as part of her natural remedies for a tribe of long-lived people near the site of origin, from whom she drinks blood as part of their healing rituals. She gives the water, and they let blood; she is sustained, and they are long-lived. She is an empath, enamored of contemporary cultures, though she interacts with humans only every 10 to 100 years. Immortals can learn from the consumption of blood and the memories written there. She maintains her childlike innocence, loves to dance, serves as a healer and prophet for her people. She always speaks in lines that mimic stairs.

3. asmeret: the older sister of iset, eldest of the sisters, second in creation. She was given immortality as a young woman. She has a passion for law, philosophy, science, and artistry. She serves as the holder of the laws of her people; they are written on her skin. She is a seeker of knowledge and has interacted with great thinkers over the ages. As a learned woman, she has often been abused, even once suffering through being flayed alive. She carries many scars. In her poems, there is always greater movement on the page. She speaks using the "I," often with asides to the gods and invocations of humanity's history.

4. enu: one of the older sisters of iset, third in creation. She serves as healer and warrior. She continues in the tradition of her people, believing deeply in the transformative and liberating power of death. Because of her dedication to learning the arts of war, she, too, has traveled widely and suffered greatly. She has no tongue. One story goes that this was cut off during the Inquisition. Another is that she removed her own tongue to prevent enemies from torturing out the secrets of another. Another is that she removed it to erase a lover's name from her body's remembrance. No one knows the truth. Her poems are always in parentheses, implying voice in silence.

5. olir: she is the younger sister of iset. She was fourth in creation and became immortal only to be with her sisters. She has no poems. She is only written about as she died early in the times of her people.

6. mae: two-spirit child of iset and her first human husband. They have always been able to speak with spirits and to be possessed by them. mae learns from spirit wisdom, distrusted by their mother and held in awe by others of the people. They always speak in tercets.

7. maat: twin of mae, daughter of iset and her human first husband. She always speaks in prose poems in connection with her mother. She was killed during a drought to keep iset alive as a human sacrifice. She possesses her twin as do other spirits. She also has the ability to move her bones and dust to communicate as her remains were never returned to the origin place and burned.

8. persephone: *daughter of iset and elisha, she is the only human. She was born of two immortals and, through the power of their genetic lines, she suffers from flashes* *of the long histories of her parents. She was raised isolated from her parents because of their insatiable thirst to appease the spirits they carry. Among her people, she is the only one to have experienced genetically transferred traumas of blackness. She is sent to a therapist who engages in gaslighting to gain her birthright: immortality.*

9. elisha: second husband of iset, also known as the second husband of god. He is a former slave from the Caribbean, created by iset as the first of her New World peoples.

10. Iblis: the devil, internal to iset and external to all.

11. Dr. Peter Decker: the only person who is not of African descent. He uses his position as a therapist to manipulate perse and gain access to source water. He becomes an immortal outside their rituals, which include a testing of the spirit, sharing of one's desires, a return to origin, and a fastening of the spirit to the body for all time. He himself starts to desiccate, because he loses his soul. He is only preserved through nonstop killing. He must be stopped. He is only written about.

12. poet: *this poet, African American and Latina woman living within this unfolding legacy of trauma in the signs of these times.*

CODE

i cannot think for all the code that shows me i am dead or not human or soon
dead or not 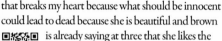 worthy or that my children will know torture written in
their cells and that our roots are steeped in blood and
there is no canopy or freedom and that no refuge
exists and that the medium is this message of split
and torn and sand what would it be to know
this in eons i cannot handle this from second to second caught up
in actions and tears and videos of my goddaughter
tap dancing and then questioning
that breaks my heart because what should be innocent
could lead to dead because she is beautiful and brown
and she is already saying at three that she likes the
white one better wants ponytails and does not like her hair or
the fox when it comes to zootopia and the bunny stereotype of
the little white woman who is prey but daring is right and
she wants to be the bunny not a fox who is predator and expected to
tear apart the prey white woman but the police will always save us and
are not to be feared though there are names and names
and names and i cannot say all of them in one breath it would take
many and so i escape into vampires no they are black immortals
because we are spirit people and have always known crossroads
and intersections and before muslim granada and its fall we were holders of
knowledge and travelers and thinkers but that was last when the world was
whole and honoring of difference but maybe it could be different so i want to
think on those who might have seen it and known such stability and
connectedness and mourned the loss and known gods in themselves
and gods by names in many languages and salt and earth and water
and what would it be to be connected to the land
not the smoke or the railroad or the machine but the land water sky
and to have it respond to your own body and the spirits within and
connected to the body and to see beyond the limits of the body
and to resist against the binary and to be ecstatic despite the mourning
and to dream a child who sees it all and grows up with it all but comes
to her own divinity and to hope that my goddaughter can see her own
divinity and humanity and worthiness there is so much code and *grito*.[1]

POET IN HERMITAGE FROM WHITENESS

how many of mine
      gurgle their jug songs

                              split house of hours

                    what is two hundred years or three or four
              stone harpoon riding whale gully in slosh & quaking

time never says its real name
      it blood-ticks and cracks teeth

                    white plaster church on a winding road

                        genocide mission in bell tolls
                            the dust whatever country

chant the names
      echo dagger chipping on bones

                            sequester water waves

                    seagull screech & spray strike
              wailing flight of child & mother bubbling mouth

                      & some will say that middle be past
              pray me silent & posed happy & minstrel laughing

how to live with denim stick
      insidious glom & never change & here

in the beginning, water sourced
the land with life: resistant fern
with its uncoiling fronds then pop
earth feathers dapple to shade
women alone controlled ember:
copper vessels polished
to sun the flame
            men always want to pit

lumina-swell behind vision screens
flutter flutter dust dance
a hip can be a still stone
when the eyes are kohl

he wanted to own the water
            young girl still playing the cool
suck from spurt
the spittle and foam

            serpent goes   he comes again with barbs

women in the round
even babes at this first birth
            bore down
            body held beneath drowning
            the suck and seep of mind
arrows through throats
flesh and crevice
screams held me down
my drowning

three days i breathed blood
before i drank
the valley desert dry

PERSEPHONE (CALL ME PERSE)

when your mother is a god
you don't get the newest goth
lipstick or bubblegum candy rings.
daughter of *mother without flaw,*
every man who sees wants to poke.
in preschool you learn about erections
from the dads circling her show and tell:
an emerald, eye-size in her palm.
mothers point their perking high,
and the teacher pats your head:
your mother tells such stories! such charm!

you get the knowing smile,
the reach of lunge anticipation–
with such a mother, what
a morsel you might be, even at 5–
        morsel: the bauble of tendon
        peeled slowly from the horrored hand
                she never deliberates violets
                when the world would show
                its cruelty to women she is perfect-cruel

and she sings so prettily to you children!
what flair, panache! i'll teach you what that means:
        his wide brown eye   thumb-sickle
        mother says be nice or she will eat
        she does anyway   peregrine falcon
swoop-gone
new doll chiseled in white

ISET, GOD AND MOTHER

all names existed within
my mother
but i cannot remember her's
it was sacred
like red mud slathered over the shaved scalp
after the rains and acacia flowers
the signs of girls blooming

my mother materials
for dung heap soil
water thatch home

in the rooms of our place
we gathered the dying
over fire and smoked herbs
from that womb
to the other place that cauls
the eyes as crossing sign

mother taught me to breathe
life : incense to burn
death : ember
or reversed?
i have forgotten the song

i never heard a care or smelled sweetness
unspoken symbiotic cycle
why doesn't my daughter know this, too?

warmth that radiated
from leather-cracked hands
how entangled her name is with vein
sacred needs
no memory to be

the spirits enveloped filled
godded me up and through
but how to be a mother and mother
to a god
when i cannot remember my own mother's name
but i see her life on my hands
and in all water
every drop of rain

PERSE AND THE HOUND

when marley juts his snout into torn quilt
i know he's sniffed me out,
he uses his nose like stubby fingers
to root his way to lick me quick and paper raw.
he angles close, beneath my arm, stays
until i give him what he wants:
scratch at the belly, pat-pat drum
while his hind leg scratches the floor,
long nails like mine would be
without bite and gnaw.

we greet this way:
early whine and paw. he knows my ache
and eases, smell of shea and sun,
particles of rolled grass in boxer short,
the only fur i love.

before, i hear him, too, guard
from the abyss edge, where
i've wine-sunk again. thin night
packed with buzz and whimper.
his nearby musk distracts,
his amber blink, its glow in tv light,
chills the tremble. he sees
so i don't.

no woman nuh cry

but freed from that torn quilt,
awake from jarring blasts,
sometimes i do i do.
too seen and wanted for more
than play-pat.

you think it is so distant   the lynching   what to make of the story my
mother told   in the car on the way to my wedding   how there was a
boy who liked her came calling round and said   *what would they do if*
we went to prom together   the white boy asked   she said *you might*
live but me they'd find in a ditch   because that's what happened to one
black boy   who went calling round a pretty white girl   the folks
warned her they warned him   but young in love defiant all that
high in the mountains   what screams to not hear   they found him
in a ditch   but her she didn't come back to town   but lived
but not so far in time   more recent still   the moroccan boy on the
edge of manhood   by the side of the road between pennsylvania and
ohio   a group of us had just returned from a conference on race and
organizing and social action hopeful not on guard   must be 14
years now   we got lost   he turned around in the wrong gravel
driveway   the man came with his gun   called the police   we
saw it   that rifle on a brown leather seat   manuel   he   held   his
hands out front   still   only reached for his wallet when the officer
said and slow   from a distance my friend david   so black and proud
went mad   we had to hold him back   so many hands   *it's not*
right it's not right   and still that officer made   manuel   go   back   to
the gravel   rake it level with bare hands   that rifle was there
while whiteness watched   while we in the next van watched   just to
know he would leave   alive   and on the day of my
wedding on the way to marry an Italian man   my mother told
a story I had heard before   a lesson was   that   ditch   still   yawning
and then a month later when we went bowling   the mountain alley
what more to do   how love noticed the whiteness   all   the
whiteness   whispered in my ear   *so white* and i said *you*
notice but i feel and my family we've been here two hundred years and him
but remember I'm the foreigner   and so we two found the lightest
ball not skilled   it was a turbulent brown we held and aimed and let go
not skilled   so many gutters waiting   next to us a couple with a
toddler i   smiled   because   children   she   smiled   back   but
him   not one word while he launched his green against the raised
guards set to guide his son's way

POET AT THE ACUPUNCTURIST

if you want a child, and one will not come
we start with needles
they may not be enough to open
you as cradle
i trust you enough to give you advice
that may unsettle others
you may have to go back
trace ancestors seven generations
learn their names
ask them to open the smoke gates
to track their own wispy bones
& guide an innocence

how many black women
can go back that far
not many
you know
the slavery of not knowing

back to the glass
behind which a record of my husband's family exists
over three centuries of women and men
a wonder
a freedom

inside my quietness
stuck with needles that hit
right at the pain radiant points
chant

heal heal heal
nameless ones i know you without
know me within
heal heal heal

my mother sent me the tree
back to Washington's scouts and slaves

with all the stories i don't know
inside crisscrossing flesh barriers
i'm not surprised in their doing

AND GOD SAID: ISET AND OLIR

i had four sisters
    whistle thorn acacia   slim needle and in pluck black ants from her teeth
        rag dance child   dry grass rattle and swirl
            the tree that strangles and is strangled
              and the one who was good

i made her to break
    she broke

to survive we must   drink
                       kill (sometimes)
                       soak in water
                       dig deep for more (more(more(moremore(...

she wanted to not want
    sought tawny veins for suck
        as if a body without a soul could be body enough
            drank so gently
            little lambs curled next to sleeping lion
            sleeping goat   just sleeping zebra
            morpheus fields   just sleeping
buzz • buzz • acidkissbuzz • buzzbuzz • maggot • eruptfly • buzz

i told her   soulless breeds soulless
i told her   life requires haunting
                 a smidgen of jugular
                 few gallons water run   no matter the cost
                                desert scrape tongue
i told her   listen to god
    she wanted twilight thrum
    quick fire dance of equator comets
    a life without hanging spirit gardens   the stench
        just husband daughter grassland tent

i told her   spirit takes

                 took

        tawny veins lead to tawny lies

        amble quickly becomes lope and paw

i told her   her arms showed pelt   her speech more bray than talk-talk

> *i took her laughing daughter, gave her ages of witness,*
> *this gift. we returned, a decade – what's time - found*
> *her in the glade, her tent, torn and blooded out. she*
> *bit her nails to flesh. i asked for her husband, the son*
> *she had just born back then when time had last been*
> *fixed by sand. i saw them, saw her son's whimper-*
> *wides as she sliced his pretty thin throat, saw her see*
> *her own self in his swallowed memories.*

i told her   she wanted

     to break

> *i took her to origin, thought the spirits would console*
> *her, sing her back to herself. she built a pyre on our*
> *waters, turned glass to catch sun spark, and sat.*
> *when she burned on the water, she was laughing.*
> *a spreading virus. her laughing daughter went to*
> *her and held. the water ran high and the rain fell*
> *deep, and i did not thirst so much. grief ? watershed.*
> *i do not know how long, how long. i forgot sand and*
> *good and sleep.*

i had four sisters

     enu   huldah   asmeret   (good has no name)

a drop and then concentric circles ripple. in each rimming valley, there is a memory, which is not yours but is you. absolute in its resonance. like watching a movie in which you are acting at that time. you are viewer and actor, but the body moving is not yours. your eyes and hands belong to you in this time and yet also belong to another time. you were crossing the street on a green light, wearing your favorite denim jeans, ripped to threading at the left thigh and the right knee. you are naked, stepping into a warm, milky bath in a tub carved into a marble floor. you smell frankincense and sweet honey; you smell a freshly run-over rat, steaming on city asphalt. a moment and you see the back of your mother's neck, thickly covered in bright torrents of beads, and you feel a rush of elation at the undulating rings, stars strung around her moving center. you know that she is your mother, but you know that she is not yours. she belongs to the other body you are inhabiting.

in a delusional disorder[2] there are several types: erotomanic; grandiose; jealous; somatic; mixed.

do you believe that a person of higher social standing is in love with you?
you only need love from me.

wind rustle. how the gilded leaf, perfect in its gold, fell upon her shoulder, loosed from her chemise. beneath goddess stares, black alabaster carved, we opened the mouth. high priestess of hidden ceremony. the body. the weeping stone. i don't know the era or country or language. today while getting blood drawn, the technician said i look more ethiopian than her, called me **አበሻ**[3] the language belonged to that time, i think.

check yourself against my words. fault is no option. bleed yourself clean.

do you believe that you have a secret, unrecognized talent? *wonder at my brilliant smile, its slow invitational peek.*

in my memories, all memories. this palm line : the first whip-cut crusted in a sea salt brine.

do you believe your partner has been unfaithful? have faith in this flint, how sharp against scalp and sin.

how many eyes did she set in a bowl for looking at other eyes? no eyes.

do you believe that you are experiencing abnormal sensations in the body or problems within the body? it is abnormal to believe what you are not told to know.

my first memory was of echoing music in the chamber of my mother's body. i've always liked prince because of those high notes releasing to sultry lows.

mixed type. twine your red yarn with my black barb until you think your veins thorned.

this reality is a delusion. just one draught of water and it all becomes clear.

so what happened today? it is all nothing. your memory is figment. you will learn to trust my story.

within a mother, ova of countless daughters and in those ova, those that may become daughters, all of the beginnings of their children. my grandmother as girl, already at her scrape of yellow bark acacia for fever and bush herbs for strength, i was already within, a tiny internal dust. i was thinking in the yellow cab.

i pray that you never | have to run again | that you do
not endure | what my neighbor did : seven guns
encircling | him weed pulling | youdearboys | broke my
glass | i found two large triangles | floor scattered
diamonds | was it sirenherald made you | adrenaline |
strained veins | i pray it made you | fearsick | will (not)
recover | never | know the glint | bullet chamber for two
| piercingfleshfear | bone like shards | i pray you receive
| blessings without | fist or brick | i pray you see | no cop
cars | tonightoranynight | that outpouring (night) | blue
glittering | blue lines | no militarized clouds | fronds
received | roughfootjumpescape | they cushioned |
soothed | brother | my brother | they called you | | — |
the ridge is just there almost there — | coinlust | for my
mechanical | nothing

POET READS THE BLOODLUST NEWS

we cannot sleep
bullet
we cannot listen to music
bullet
we cannot technicolor dream
bullet
we cannot go to space
bullet
we cannot marry
bullet
we cannot have children
bullet
our children cannot play
bullet
our mothers cannot seek help
bullet
our fathers cannot be tall
bullet
our grandmothers cannot open doors
bullet
our grandfathers cannot remember
bullet
we cannot vote
bullet
we cannot eat
bullet
we cannot be
be bullet

DEFINING PERSEPHONE

you wonder why an african
would name you death harbinger
make you sign your name
                    in greek
                        architecture of letters that meld with your hand
so many iterations of othering
                            who conquers newborn skin

you want to know why she collars you   springtime
future harvest   colors: black for eyes   manteca baby
            what does reaping feel like
why god lusts for stains   spilt merlot

            whose death will you be bringing
                                    sometimes you open mouth
and only lapis cords unfurl   river solid around body chunks
so yours you feel the quickening explosion   fire synapse slaughter song
            neuron wants to tell you   i want to tell you before i
                                        eye death

you wonder if you were kidnapped
        from brutal love that holds a baby hostage for thank you and please
you never say (those) things   does gratitude sweeten the tongue sour

you want to be kore-chiseled
        witness/numb/stone
unseeing   how eyes roll to white   no one thinks to close

always open pools on this face
                trumpet announcement of rage bull   this tempo-loosed heart

~NOT SUPPOSED TO BE: ISET ON BIRTHING UNWANTED, BLUE, THEN ALIVE

~   describable

~   indigo brown beneath filmcaul
             spiraling comet trail graced on skin
             her veins a nightroot system
~   a room this silent

she defies our lust for pumping

              ~   tick tick clock stuck on 47 tick

within wonderworker hands
~   elisha breathes whirl down
~   lapis cracks and here pulsepink

         ~   she was never supposed to be my dark mirror
                    looking through shadow glass
                           like crinoline
                      over sheeted eyes

     enu mouthed kule[4] precious giving
her name came seed and sprout
her name came crash and breathless

~   sin came *l'appel du vide*[5]

           ~   teeth broken on silk skin

~   that he loved her
           why couldn't I in un(mother)ing

~   and *cafuné*[6] to mimic soft
           have I birthed water or rock

           ~   *ya'aburnee*[7] unbearable self

POET: ON IMAGINING PLANET X AS THE ONLY
SAFE SPACE

sandy
laquan
gynnya
trump the death card. the joker. the torture wheel.

walls rise tall
with bricks inlaid with suspended orbits
i'm packing my spacesuit and i'm taking my shit and moving to the moon
where there are no rules[8]
monáe I hear your painted star exhale to mechanized

stop my heart
coldcoldstop
unbearable peaking
beat hop through rib
metalbreakflesh

casings

packing my spacesuit and moving to dark
planet   an ice theory for this nemesis

implacable justice my scheme
if blessing comes in brown bodies surrounded in chalk
what from the necessary curse
fanon
packing my spacesuit
revolution is carving whiteness from my own flesh
tyche's anticolonial antimanifest antioppression but destiny
entanglement
bangbangsplatter

loosie[9] suspicions
lynching after styx

take me to the ice
not the water

cameras watch
but no one sees a thing
don't look for brown skin flecks to mine
and stitch for a fancy new sunburn suit
melanin envy
but shoot the bearer

rocket ember   shot liberation

moving moving

where the rooms rise to capture
and light dances in blink wink still alive

what happened to

name

name

name
empty seats on a rocket
countdown ... 7 [10] ... 18 [11] ... 16 [12] ... 28 [13] ... 17 [14] ... 25 [15] ... 12 [16] ... 43 [17]
challenge(r)

PERSE'S NIGHTMARE

you are on a bus
in front of you are all these coworkers
it's a team-building trip
you head to a castle with a medieval façade
but inside an elevator.
it takes you and all these people down
        down down stop and let someone off
        down down down stop and two go
        repeat repeat repeat
at the bottom it's just you
and you

                                        me and peter

everyone waits above where green grass burns so bright!
but you have to make your way up
through horror floors

                                grimace faces frozen in melt
                                reaching hands with barbs for fingers
                                fanning swords that glint peacock eyes

you want refuge

                                        peter laughing
                                            doubt

you look up
the staircase
impatient for turquoise and spring
        up up up

                                            no end

rippling shadow in the eaves

POET ON WATCHING HER LOVER GARDEN
PERSEPHONE'S DREAM

we must do what we are meant / wait within unfurling green
lemoncurls / nibbled by aphids but healed in stretch / open
the windows to jasmine in mouth

| | he has lost his cap & captures it fast / before claiming spirit somersault | |

wake white pear flower / adored by his wonder / your leaves
giggle soft in bay wind / i know this soundflutter / each
morning i know / it tastes like buzzhop & sweet /
the half full bear on porcelain coasters / grips his frozen
jiggle belly / i wink for his beady black eyes /

we were eden once / the first ones with vines for veins /
entangled in the passionflower / mouths bursting in fig /
you do not know his secret / the fire mark still
on his hip /

meant to tend / him-now to sedum coils / between spiked
aloe / healing healing   allahealing / i haven't seen
a snail / in the mirror for weeks

PERSE: A LAST SUMMER

in the way that some are lasts
you bask in the small details
                ashen wood creaks, rough hewn planks on bare feet
                made of braided and sewn rags
                burns on his hands
                ceramic and glass that carved black
                tear drops in splatter at thumb crevice
                when he turned them up
                thick callouses
                mound smooth

you remember the scrape
as he held
to go to the yellowed cave: faded
wallpaper and a bed that spanned
the fullness of the space
a rickety nightstand
vessel for game

gather the tools
then the low table
more like halved barrel
for moonshine or bathing

                                                            season depending

above it, his butter cream
setting hazel eyes
you call him picky

                                                            and this is his good name

he teaches you poker
but not poker
first shuffling technique
how to hold the hand

as if pouring lemonade
from two painted pitchers

you hold your thumbs at the handles
curve your fingers to press
to wood with cards between
flesh and grain then run

                          a sound like library pages turning
                      or radio static in between chill mountains

you taptap to stack the cards in order
after the sputter to cataclysm you make
he builds a bridge
lets go and blends

                                 his voice
                            after the last summer?

just the light of window slats
far from that day and that chill
when the tulip tree pinks
clustered in blossoms
that scattered all over the neighborhood

                        this always happens near your birthday

how you practiced the summer
then fall and winter and spring
before you got it right

                                 the bridge

and you didn't know where it was going
though it burned

POET ANXIETY DISORDER

i know he loves me when i panic
we are trying to leave an outkast
concert & so is everyone else
throngs from five different stages
bottlerock   bottleneck
one exit for thousands

i see a baby while i count
like i have practiced
first spanish portuguese french
i always get stuck in the 80s then
remember up and down
zero to 100

                                                    back

how many men
how many cell phones
how many beer bottles
how many light bulbs

how many black people
i don't go too far up

i ask him to teach me italian
count zero to 200
up down twice   i make jokes
it's a defense mechanism
to keep breathing
not feel
jab throb encroachment

i come from a place where every elbow means fight

> white people do not consider the war of space
> too used to having so much
> not having to fight for so little

i sometimes deal in generalities

> i am naming it
> i am panicking be
> cause we are not free
> no escape
> no exit

i can't see a way

flap my arms like a blackbird

> *i want out i just want a way out just let me out out out out!*

almost hit another woman
hold arms close
rockhold
tears burn & track

he holds his arms out
protects my space
begins to rage at the white woman volunteer
who calls into a useless walkie-talkie

> *we have a medical emergency*

she wants me to go back to the stands
to breathe in capture   display a body alone
> dark sky standing on a barren field
> *i'm ok we are almost there i just need to see a way*

i know he loves me when i panic

| ~ |

> in an email
> *all lives matter*

45

in an email
I asked my seven black grandchildren and they told me I'm right: postracial
in an email
when you criticize an administrator by name, it's scary

whose discourse is preserved in plaintive civility
i can't be racist, i have a black friend
a black grandchild
& then
some have called me racist

i count the emails
english spanish portuguese french italian
get stuck in numbers
like when i was black (invisible) child
stuck counting tiles in a diner while adults chatted after church
or later the checks in a man's tie
when he said   *you're not as beautiful as you think you are*
& later still when i drive to work
i feel panic rise again
surrounded by trees
          count the trees
knot in

PERSEPHONE JUDGED

you know freedom comes gentle
      enu: thin blades   thread
      hulda: mica eyes   smoothing hand grace
      asmeret: all stories stippled into papyrus skin
      iset: cannot find
           good in

you
      know they have burnt
his tree   petrified body   sulfur flash poof

                        bye bye love

when they come with razor-edged scoop
you open wide   myrrh resin shine
you quake your shell
stuff your own mouth with cotton

                       right eye watch

left
                  memory suck so they know
                       how wanting

silence seen
                       burned first

no matter
      dissemble

      for cosmesis they will pierce
      the rim redredreddot
you expect motion parallax   quick closing of flicker smiles
     slowing in vision fields of yesteryear   how they fade away
you know that you wanted
      relative flatness   escape from contour overlays
         how many count-sore ways can blackness be devoured
         how many sweat drill traumas can be endured
            no sunset over still island
            no baby step in pepper and salt sand

no shimmer through lacey veil
no pucker press sweetened by mango
no tempering

you know you are wrong
liberation requires your damning

there was a storm, but not a squall that twists bodies like
mangled steel around a pristine-perfect trellis; it was
trouble-hue that shakes death dice until smooth palms
turn calloused & snake eyes bleed maggots through
black. that was how s√he loved, in slip-tongue forking
through ear to tease sense into dull passion-quake, &
when sense pried itself back, s√he had a crowbar
answer. oh, s√he loved that way, too. devil likes you to
hallelujah-talk *baby*, or *slick*, or everything you'll never
have. that's just the way justice be. when s√he loses you,
it will be because s√he's sniffing another blood trail.
s√he's been jealous of wriggling babes for eons. when
s√he loses your sweat on tongue, your spent body
slumped against glass, s√he was never there at all. you
just imagined that spirit, clever blaze. blame glory
cannonade thumping heart or empty house haunting.
blame possession & angels & demons & that one movie
you watched that convinced you that shadows stalked.
when s√he loses you, don't worry; s√he's still close.
those thin ticking fingers know tap of your hipbones by
the hurt; s√he plays other music as diversion like you, a
grim percussion aria. & smile toothy clean. you made
your claim to pock, & still moon s&s shifted. s√he never
bore a scar but you.

it ends with a bullet to the head
                    or a sickle   machete   spiked bat
any dead-em will do

                              livor mortis   rigor mortis   algor mortis
                    body cools blood stains the skin fixed in its timelessness
                              days it takes to blacken
                    first the extending green divines rotting flesh
                                        some gods blue & some gods kelp
                         purple bruise & then black
                              that's real

only movies go   bite + time = skin slip & black spurt

                         in truth
                    eyes protrude & challenge tongue
                    intestines reveal their tangle
                    push through vagina & rectum

black people have no futures
in sci-fi or horror

                                        white man apocalypse :
                                        whiteness grays & turns black
                                        crow black eyes or embalmed roll-white

we always die first in the movies
when death leads to
black running

                                        how dare those zombies crave
                                                beasts
                                        everyone needs a cure

it all ends with a bullet
& a bonfire
zombies aren't human

                    consciousness ripples

i give you
mercy[18]

i keep searching my head for holes
               practicing,   *stop. don't shoot.*   *i'm alive.*

NOTES

1. Shout in Spanish
2. "Delusional Disorder" as described by *Psychology Today*
3. Amharic, meaning "carried child on the back" or "carried fruits (tree)," pronounced *āzele*
4. Milk in the Maasai language
5. Literally translated as the call of the void in French, but describes an instinctive desire to jump from heights.
6. Brazilian Portuguese work for tenderly running fingers through someone's hair
7. Is an Arabic declaration of the hope of leaving the earth before a beloved, because it is impossible and unbearable to imagine living without this one.
8. Reference to "Sally Ride" as sung by Janelle Monáe
9. Loosie is a reference to loose cigarettes
10. Age of Aiyana Stanley-Jones when she was killed while sleeping
11. Age of Michael Brown when he was killed
12. Age of Gynnya McMillen when she died.
13. Age of Sandra Bland when she was killed
14. Age of Laquan McDonald when he was killed
15. Age of Freddie Gray when he was killed
16. Age of Tamir Rice when he was killed
17. Age of Eric Garner when he was killed
18. "I give you mercy" is a reference to *Z Nation*, a television series on SyFy that follows a group of travelers, led by a Black woman, as they face and attempt to stop a zombie apocalypse.

ACKNOWLEDGEMENTS

The author gratefully acknowledges the women of the Bay Area Writing Workshop for granting a few critical eyes and much support to the work. Finally, great thanks to the arts communities of Acentos, Cave Canem, CantoMundo, the Carolina African American Writers Collective, Cleave: Bay Area Women Writers, the Saint Mary's MFA Program (particularly my chair, Brenda Hillman, and reader, Geoffrey O'Brien), Macondo, and the Bay Area writing community for providing the spaces to write and to hear the work in the world.

Acknowledgements are also due to the journals in which some of the poems from this collection first appeared: *Aster(ix):* "poet: rigor mortis, zombies, & dehumanization"; *Bozalta:* "poet: on imagining Planet X as the only safe space"; *Fourteen Hills:* "olire and mire"; *New Madrid:* "poet in hermitage from whiteness"; *Obsidian: Literature and Arts in the African Diaspora Journal:* "vial two and after the cinema"; *Remembering the Days that Breathed Pink:* "(what to do"; *Torch:* "when your mother is a god, vessel strut, salvage yard"; *Vitriol:* "lilith snake beloved," "at origin," "amor ciego," "bringing death," (what to do."

RAINA J. LEÓN, PhD, Cave Canem graduate fellow (2006), CantoMundo graduate fellow (2016), Macondista, and member of the Carolina African American Writers Collective, has been published in numerous journals as a writer of poetry, fiction, and nonfiction. She is the author of three collections of poetry, *Canticle of Idols, Boogeyman Dawn,* and *sombra: (dis)locate* (2016). She has received fellowships and residencies with the Kimmel Harding Nelson Center for the Arts, Montana Artists Refuge, the Macdowell Colony, Ragdale, the Tyrone Guthrie Center in Annamaghkerrig, Ireland, and the Vermont Studio Center. She also is a founding editor of *The Acentos Review*, an online quarterly, international journal devoted to the promotion and publication of LatinX arts and writing. She is an associate professor of education at Saint Mary's College of California.